VALOUR, LOVE AND LIFE

POEMS JOURNEYING PLACES, TIME, BATTLES, LOVE AND LAUGHTER

AF565535

DIVYA KHANDURI

Copyright © Divya Khanduri
All Rights Reserved.

ISBN 979-888569200-7

This book has been published with all efforts taken to make the material error-free after the consent of the author. However, the author and the publisher do not assume and hereby disclaim any liability to any party for any loss, damage, or disruption caused by errors or omissions, whether such errors or omissions result from negligence, accident, or any other cause.

While every effort has been made to avoid any mistake or omission, this publication is being sold on the condition and understanding that neither the author nor the publishers or printers would be liable in any manner to any person by reason of any mistake or omission in this publication or for any action taken or omitted to be taken or advice rendered or accepted on the basis of this work. For any defect in printing or binding the publishers will be liable only to replace the defective copy by another copy of this work then available.

To all who have brought us peace

And walked alongside, to smoothen the crease,

To calm the whirlwind in our minds and stirred

The souls to let our songs be heard

Contents

1. Books

The musty pages and the frayed bound cover
Relays a story we must uncover
To disappear from the worldly calling
And set foot in a world so enthralling.
Are you here to witness the magic within?
These pages are doors, let the adventure begin.
Soon you'll be treading with the characters you meet
Welcoming you aboard the cobbled street.
You'll laugh and cry, be merry to make them your own
Such joyous hours you have never known
As you totter along the epochs of time
You'd often wonder why it feels so sublime.
It does, by virtue of the charm in the words
Crafted for flight like the wings of the birds.
As you fly higher into the sun-kissed sky
You'd never pause to question why.
Why must this story cease?
Within it, you found your release
But you thank and revere, this wonder that is a book
And prance to forge your personal reading nook.

2. Grandfather

We live their lives through our eyes
Knowing what we can see
Above the support of the aging knees
Lies a wisp of uncertainty.
While we fall back in time
They laugh at our childish rhymes
And today we look into their tired eyes
To see the love that never lies.
The love that wished us health and wealth
The love that gave us all in stealth
The love that persists through all this time
Yearning to give more all the while.
It's their care and love we'd miss the most
It's their opinion on matters we'd like to accost
Only to realize they are pure of heart
Showing unwavering love from the start.
While they paved a path for our joy and quests
Forgetting it was us who are blessed
With such a wonderful man we thought we knew
While he sat in that sunlit view..
His shadow enveloping us in the warmth and hue
Of shades of love in which we grew.
He might be feeble and sits in silence

But he'll not cease to be a valence
To our joy and aspiration and hearts desires
Shielding us from these raging fires.
So while we may feel worry and fleeting sorrow
Know that there is a morrow
Where he still loves us for how we quell
The wisp of uncertainty on which he no longer dwells.

3. Rise

Fearing the mist of the future
We live in the shadows of our past
Ignoring the warmth of the present
Becoming the light that'll never last.
The fleeting moments of joy that surround us
Never summon the question why
They lull us into a complacent view thus
Making the answer not worth the try.
Why do we embroider our lives
With tales of wonder and light
Only to hasten the darkness
Falling with that unyielding might.
What did we gain from sorrows in our past
No wiser did we become today
What did we gain with the unwanted foray
Into the memories which are forever lost.
I only wish we did more
More to find the truth
More to face our fears
More to strengthen our minds
And our souls
More to make us whole.
I only wish we could do more

More to hasten our rise
From ashes of the darkest gray
To a phoenix in the blue skies.

4. Our Furry Friend

They set the timber basket on the deck
It carried a note that was merely a speck
We opened it to reveal a slant of ink
It read "He'll love you most", signed off with a wink.
I rushed to shove the lid away
For what peered out, yes, it made our day
With furry paws and those little deep eyes
We stood back and heaved a sigh.
He whined and made our hearts but melt
Such pure love we had never felt
I lift him up and he proceeds to sniff
He's making me his, as he catches a whiff..
A whiff of us, to remember us by
To snuggle in, whenever we cry
He yearns for those pets and nuzzles
Through silent nights and the daily hustle.
He loves you most, while you look away
Barks and wags his tail, as if to say
"I'll be with you through it all,
Wherever you may shine or fall."
His heart just beats for you indeed
He ages faster, be he any breed
As he grows old, he devotes his time

To await your return, without caring a dime.
While his paws still engulf your heart with warmth
This bond lasts forever, from when it's formed
And I cradle him, he sniffs, turns his eyes to mine
"Don't just cry, I am completely fine."
And as he hops to another world
My furry friend, I sit with him, all curled
We sob and reminisce the time gone by
Kiss his nose, to bid a teary goodbye.
For he gifted us, a love so true
To be blessed with him, we were the fortuitous few
We now sniff to catch a whiff of his coat
It's just wisps but our lives he re-wrote.

5. Beauty

Sitting amidst the snow clad peaks
Looking up at the bluest of skies
Where might I find
A sound so pure
Which would help us all rise?
And then I hear your voice
In the distant thoughts that I seem to have read
I let out a sigh and smile knowing you laughed
At the simple words I said.
What's peace for you, holds true for me
An abundance of joy for you, is what I'd want to see
For I feel blessed to not just have met you
I feel blessed, for the journey that we are wading through.
What must this mean for the two of us
A confluence of words, emotions, love and joy?
While seemingly quiet but resounding with thoughts to share
As we move along this winding path, I am grateful that we both do care.

6. Bravehearts of the Soil

They know not what fear is
And embrace it with open arms
Turning it to valor at their behest
Never failing to leave a mark,
In our hearts and our souls
They leave no stone unturned
And protect us in the dark.
As the shadows crawl in the valleys
Casting ominous signs in the twinkling starlight
Oh, bear witness to this irony of beauty
Amidst the wondrous stars, see the light of their plight!
The stream from the glacier wants to lull them to sleep
Cradle them with her gentle sounds, and to rid them of their dreams.
She tries to meander, welcoming these brave sons who soar
Not knowing their spirit to be buried at her shores.
While they fight, fist, gun and knives
Craving for the last hugs from their daughters, mothers and wives,
Shielding their brothers, they gasp for air and fall
Never in their lives have these men felt so tall.
Do we peer over our shoulders, terrified of the unknown?
No. These men trudged through snow, through toil

To protect us, to etch their names so we never forget
The bravehearts of the soil.

7. Judge

A gentle nudge
Through the daily trudge
To pause, not be raring to judge.
What makes right, right
Do we feel the plight
Of another man's darkest night?
Can we pay heed
To this man's need
And to forget his horrendous deed?
Can we beckon his life
Away from strife
That forced him to wield that knife?
What must we do
For these cross roads are true
To influence the power of few?
As we seethe in anger
And hold dear the rancour
The hatred alas! gets anchored,
In the wild seas
That ask us to flee
While the fettered man voices his plea.
Can he be virtuous
After a night so tumultuous

To rebuild the dark into light so mellifluous.
Let's give him a chance
And take a stance
To let him live another dance.

8. Saving my Brothers in Arms

As I trudge along in knee deep snow
Amidst mountains rising into the sky
I try to imagine a faint deep glow
From the place where my brothers lie...
... in wait as we a team of twenty men strong
Try to read the direction which may be wrong.
It all began when nature went against us
Carrying afloat a heptor to a valley unknown thus
With three men aboard with no way out
We brothers in arms were called to scout.
With fear in our hearts and courage in our souls
We set out into this flighty temptress, the night
The gales too strong, and the blizzard raining down
There isn't a moment to stop and frown.
Do we know where our next step leads?
To valleys of snow or crevasses so deep.
Are we hailed as superhuman?
Who can conquer all land, water, skies and mountain
Or are we are just given this significance
For others to escape this encumbrance?
But we decide to bear either weapon or extra shoes to pair
Our fettered uniforms with no steering light

Can you imagine, my brothers, our plight?
Remember us for the camaraderie we bestow
You would only know, of this story when shown
The relentless shower of hail and snow, in the mountains and valleys so deep and cold..
And you have to trudge with frozen feet
Not knowing where your next step leads.

9. Accept the Mist

These empty roads and misty trails
Ensnare our souls to set them on sail
On rough waters with no land in sight
Merging with yet another cold and starless night.
The moonlit night and wondrous pines
Casting shadows and whispering signs
Leading us to quieter shores
Quivering at what lies in store.
Here we glimpse forgotten lands
With slight footprints on retreating sands
Welcoming tides on this wondrous night
Offering the strength to rise and fight.
Look here! Listen to what the gale sings
Unfolding a riveting tale, it give us wings
As the music helps us brave our thoughts
We witness what our mind is not.
And it's not a person on its own
It is what we have always known
A part of you, a part of me
And that is what sets us free.
As our past hovers below this starless night
It does so, to rid us of our plight
While gazing with wonder at the moon's crescent

We smile, accepting the mist in our present.

10. Winter

The tinted windows shone pearly bright
It made for such a calming sight
As the drops of rain pattered on the sill
The hourglass and our lives stood very still.
Glancing at the hazy shapes
Through the windows we see the flakes
The rain welcomes its colder chum
Singing a melody, we'd love to hum.
Can we hear those larks gently trill?
Flying atop the glistening hill
Confessing their love for the cascading snow
Beckoning us for us to know..
The tender warmth the cold does bestow
Emboldened with the fallen snow
It binds a spell with all its charm
As we peer out, arm in arm.
Step out into the frosty night
Boulevards coloured with sparkly white
Accost the snow which gleams so bright
Embrace the winter with amaranthine flight.

11. Music

Why do we dance to the slightest beat
And swirl and sway and tap our feet
It is indeed the warmest chortle
Forging valor to meet the hurdle.
It may be played on drums and harps
A prelude of poignant flats and sharps
Resounding in our hearts and souls
Rallying all to make us whole.
It hops through cultures and different worlds
Making kids, in joyous laughter, twirl
To merry songs from beyond the sea
Crafted melodies to welcome the jubilee.
Hark, the message this music bears
To rid us all of imagined fears
We are the same, no matter the tongue
Let's sing the song that's still unsung.

12. Words at Night

Words held together with threads so fine
Laden with love and colors that shine
Painting these nights into patterns that place
Our worlds within an eternal grace.
The dim lights scattered across the valley
Often come together to rally
The cause, the emotion, the love, the care
To be ever so grateful for the time we share.
Oh! Heed these wisps of twinkling lights
Leading us home in the darkest of nights
Along streams that gush down this winding hill
We halt and remain ever so still.
Let's listen to these woods so deep
The pines that whisper and will forever keep
Our laughter echoing in their midst
Our joyous words rising from the mist..
Words that cherish, and revere and mould
Our thoughts and actions, to make us whole.

9 798885 692007

Printed by Libri Plureos GmbH in Hamburg, Germany